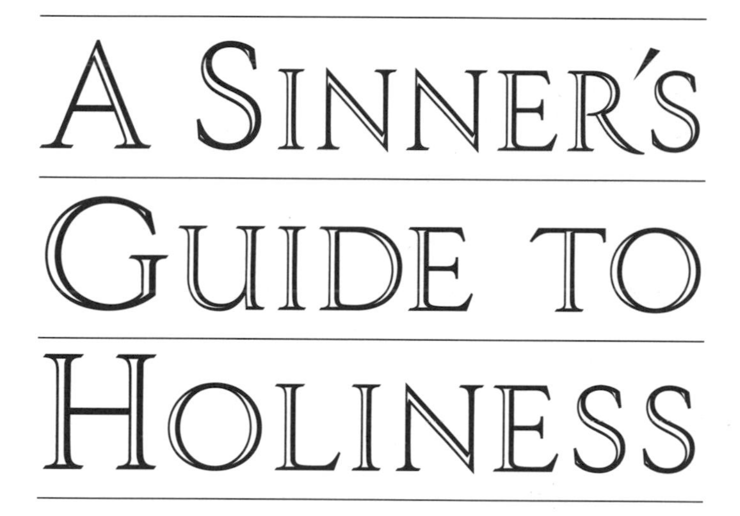

John Chapman

Guidebooks for Life

Bible-based essentials
for your Christian journey

A Sinner's Guide to Holiness is the first in a new series of straightforward, practical Christian books from Matthias Media. As the series unfolds, it will deal with the important, nuts-and-bolts topics that Christians need to know about as we walk each day with our Master.

Some Christian books are all theory and no practical application; others are all stories and tips with no substance. The Guidebooks for Life will aim to achieve a vital balance—that is, to dig into the Bible and discover what God is telling us there, as well as applying that truth to our daily Christian lives.

For up-to-date information about the latest Guidebooks for Life, visit our website: www.matthiasmedia.com.au

GUIDEBOOKS FOR LIFE

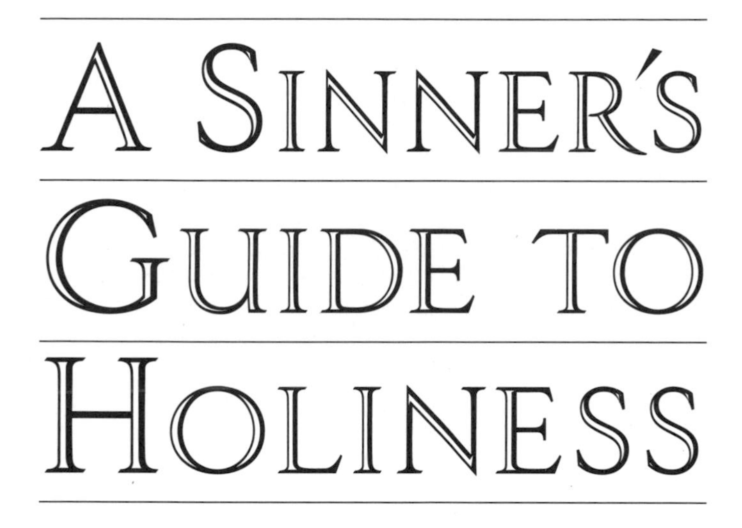

A SINNER'S GUIDE TO HOLINESS

'HOLINESS' MAY SEEM A LONG WAY OFF. BUT GOD HAS A PLAN FOR GETTING YOU THERE.

John Chapman

matthiasmedia

A Sinner's Guide to Holiness

Matthias Media
(St Matthias Press Ltd. ACN 067 558 365)
PO Box 225
Kingsford NSW 2032 Australia
Telephone: (02) 9663 1478; international: +61-2-9663-1478
Facsimile: (02) 9663 3265; international: +61-2-9663-3265
Email: info@matthiasmedia.com.au
Internet: www.matthiasmedia.com.au

ISBN 1 921068 08 6

Cover design and typesetting by Lankshear Design Pty Ltd.
Printed in Hong Kong

My thanks to Tony Payne from Matthias Media for suggesting to me that a new generation needed to hear the timeless biblical message of holiness, and for encouraging me to write this book. I am also very grateful to my good friend Michael Orpwood, who read the manuscript, turned the sentences into English, and made helpful comments.

CONTENTS

HOLINESS

1. Where it begins

I SUPPOSE IF YOU ARE anything like me your attitude to holiness goes something like this: "Oh God, make me holy, but not too holy and not too soon."

Lurking deep down inside each of us is the thought that if we were to be made holy, in the way that God is holy, then there could well be some things we very much want for ourselves from which we would be excluded. We would miss out on something good that we could otherwise have. We fear that God may call on us to do something we will hate. We suspect, half-unconsciously, that God may not have our best interests at heart after all. He may interrupt our quest for money, or for popularity, or for success, to our great loss and disadvantage.

This thinking, although natural, is of course wrong, and it is one basic reason why there is such an urgent need for us to consider the subject of holiness. One major purpose of writing this book is simply to remind us again that "no good thing does [the LORD] withhold from those who walk uprightly" (Ps 84:11). To be holy—that is, to be like God in character—is to live the 'good life'.[1] If we desire to live that good life, then our understanding of this subject should not be considered an optional extra. We should read on. Even more importantly, we should pray for understanding of holiness and pray that God will indeed cause us to be holy.

What is holiness?

What then is holiness? Holiness is a term that is regularly used not of people but of God. He is often referred to as "the Holy One of Israel".[2] The idea behind such a title is that God is entirely other, distinct and separate from everything he has made.

When the word 'holiness' is used in connection with God, it's a bit like an expanding suitcase. The more you know about him, the bigger the concept of holiness becomes—and the more meaning you

1 John 10:10

2 This reference occurs mainly in the Psalms and Isaiah. See, for example, Psalm 71:22, 78:41 and 89:18, and Isaiah 1:4, 5:19 and 24, 10:20, 12:6, 17:7, 29:19, 30:11, 12 and 15, 31:1, etc.

discover is packed into this one word 'holiness'. Because God is great, speaking of his holiness is to open up a massive subject where we will discover that we see in part rather than in whole. This should not put us off, however. If we really reached the point where we thought we'd comprehended everything there is to know about God, there is also a very good chance that we would be getting it wrong.

I want to consider two essential characteristics of God's holiness. I want to consider, firstly, God's holiness as power and might. Secondly, I want to consider God's holiness in terms of his perfect purity.

Holiness as power and might

God is holy—separate, distinct, and other—in his power and in his might. He is not the same as us. We must realize from the outset that he is different; and different in that he is far greater and more powerful than either we could be or we could even hope to grasp hold of.

This difference or separateness—this *holiness*—is well illustrated in the book of Job. The book of Job is named after its principal character, and, except for a bit at the beginning and a bit at the end, it is simply a long poem. It opens with a good man who, as well as being good, is also healthy, wealthy and wise. He has a large family, and his many children are a source of great delight to their father. Into the bargain we may add that Job is godly—something that the writer of Job is at pains to insist on from the very beginning.[3]

However, in one fell swoop the wheels completely fall off Job's semitrailer. Job's property is plundered and stolen. His houses burn down. All his children are killed in an accident. His health fails. He himself becomes so sick and so badly disfigured that when his three friends visit him they can hardly recognize that it is Job.

Job's three friends are so distressed at the sight they see, that after a period of silence (which is their most helpful contribution) they feel obligated to make some theological reflections on his condition and position. They sum up the situation, and suggest to Job that his present troubles must be because of God's judgement on him for something very sinful that he has done. Job immediately protests that he isn't any more sinful than they are. They all feel the need to speak, however, and their message is fairly uniform. They speak one at a time and Job answers them each time. So while they only have to speak once, he has to answer three times. It is a long and tedious process he has to go through, as he hears the same arguments again and again from three slightly different, but essentially identical, perspectives.

Because all three friends take the same wrong-headed line, by the end of the conversations Job has been almost driven to distraction. His suffering has

3 Indeed, the point about Job's righteousness is made by God himself in Job 1:8.

been greatly compounded. He knows that what they are saying is totally incorrect; he sees that their theological understanding of the situation is simplistic, and that it has completely missed the mark. The three friends put us in mind of the saying that for every complex problem there is a simple solution—a solution that is almost certainly wrong.

I almost forgot to tell you that when all three friends have finally worn themselves out, yet another friend comes and sticks his oar into the discussion. He adds nothing new, but manages to intensify Job's suffering by underlining and repeating what all the others have already said.

In chapter 23 of the book, we read as follows:

> Then Job answered and said:
>
> "Today also my complaint is bitter;
> my hand is heavy on account of my groaning.
> Oh, that I knew where I might find him,
> that I might come even to his seat!
> I would lay my case before him
> and fill my mouth with arguments.
> I would know what he would answer me
> and understand what he would say to me.
> Would he contend with me in the greatness of
> his power?
> No; he would pay attention to me.
> There an upright man could argue with him,
> and I would be acquitted forever by my judge."
> (Job 23:1-7)

Here, Job seems to be very close to blasphemy. "If I could find God, I would have it out with him" is what he is saying. It is almost as if he views himself as God's equal.

This seems to me to be the inevitable result of Job accepting, at least in part, the wrong theology he is being told by his friends. Wrong theology always results in wrong behaviour. It is one reason why we should not despise the study of theology, as if it doesn't matter what we believe. It is also a very good reason why we should pray regularly for those who teach us about God, and why we should study the Bible for ourselves with great diligence and care.

The book of Job continues for quite a few more chapters. Job's friends persist with their simplistic line of theology, and Job continues stubbornly to respond that he is completely innocent of any wrongdoing.

Eventually, and after all have said their piece to the point of exhaustion, God appears to Job.

When reading the book of Job for the first time I remember thinking, "Surely, now that God has appeared, he will be able to say that Job was right all along, and that his friends were in the wrong". It seems only right and fair, given what Job has suffered. But if this seems the obvious response on God's part, we are in for a great surprise. God's response doesn't follow the expected pattern at all. It appears, indeed, that there is a far more important matter that needs immediate attention, and God has appeared in order to address it.

Then the LORD answered Job out of the whirlwind
and said:

> "Who is this that darkens counsel by words
> without knowledge?
> Dress for action like a man;
> I will question you, and you make it known
> to me. (Job 38:1-3)

I must say that to have God speak to me in this way would have made me feel extremely apprehensive. When I am told to 'brace myself like a man', I never imagine that what is about to happen will be a relaxing or pleasant experience. And indeed, God's cross-examination of Job is very 'heavy roller' treatment. God begins by asking Job if he was present with him, helping him, when he created the cosmos.

> "Where were you when I laid the foundation of
> the earth?
> Tell me, if you have understanding.
> Who determined its measurements—surely you know!
> Or who stretched the line upon it?
> On what were its bases sunk,
> or who laid its cornerstone,
> when the morning stars sang together
> and all the sons of God shouted for joy?
>
> "Or who shut in the sea with doors
> when it burst out from the womb,
> when I made clouds its garment
> and thick darkness its swaddling band,

and prescribed limits for it
and set bars and doors,
and said, 'Thus far shall you come, and no farther,
and here shall your proud waves be stayed'?

"Have you commanded the morning since your
  days began,
and caused the dawn to know its place,
that it might take hold of the skirts of the earth,
and the wicked be shaken out of it?
It is changed like clay under the seal,
and its features stand out like a garment.
From the wicked their light is withheld,
and their uplifted arm is broken." (Job 38:4-15)

"Can you bind the chains of the Pleiades
or loose the cords of Orion?
Can you lead forth the Mazzaroth in their season,
or can you guide the Bear with its children?
Do you know the ordinances of the heavens?
Can you establish their rule on the earth?

"Can you lift up your voice to the clouds,
that a flood of waters may cover you?
Can you send forth lightnings, that they may go
and say to you, 'Here we are'?
Who has put wisdom in the inward parts
or given understanding to the mind?
Who can number the clouds by wisdom?
Or who can tilt the waterskins of the heavens,
when the dust runs into a mass
and the clods stick fast together?" (Job 38:31-38)

It is a long speech; the longest in the book so far, and it is not over yet. God continues in this way for the rest of this and the following two chapters. It is totally and utterly overwhelming.

Listen then to how Job reacts to these words of God. This time, we are not at all surprised to find that the Job who speaks is a very different man from the one who first demanded that God would appear and give him justice.

> Then Job answered the LORD and said:
>
> "I know that you can do all things,
> and that no purpose of yours can be thwarted.
> 'Who is this that hides counsel without knowledge?'
> Therefore I have uttered what I did not understand,
> things too wonderful for me, which I did not know.
> 'Hear, and I will speak;
> I will question you, and you make it known to me.'
> I had heard of you by the hearing of the ear,
> but now my eye sees you;
> therefore I despise myself,
> and repent in dust and ashes." (Job 42:1-6)

As Job is presented with the greatness and awe of God's majesty, he says something not too far different from, "I am little, and you are big. Little people shouldn't tell big people where to get off". That is, he has said what he should not have said, and he now humbly repents of stepping over this line.

One thing noticeably absent from God's speech is

this: Job receives no immediate answer to the question 'Why?' The reason for his suffering is not given. He does not even learn at this point whether he or his friends were right in their assessment of his condition and its causes. Rather, his question fades into the background, lost and forgotten in the face of the *otherness* of God, his holiness, greatness, and power.

Because of this, we must conclude that Job's 'repentance' is not because of some moral sin, obvious or hidden. He repents not for some specific wrong thing that he has done in the past, but because he has failed to treat God as he deserves. In his speech-making, he had made his demands as if he and God were almost equals. Now he is reminded, and has come to terms with the reality, that he is not able to demand God's action. God is God, and Job is not. Job is to relate to God as God really is, not as an equal. Job is to relate to God in full recognition that God is infinitely greater than Job in power, might and holiness.

This in turn demonstrates a very important aspect of our response to the holiness of God.

During the course of my ministry I have met unbelievers who say to me, "I would become a follower of Jesus provided that he would do such and such"; or "I would start believing in God if only he would fulfil this condition or provide this or that proof". This thinking is both foolish and wrong-headed. It demonstrates that the one speaking has simply not come to terms with God's holiness. The fact of the matter is that God is God and we are not. We are his creatures, nothing more. We are not the Creator, and we have no right to impose any terms or conditions upon him or upon the nature of his existence, or upon the way he must behave towards us.

It is part of the extraordinary blindness of humans that we persist in believing the lie—first perpetrated in the Garden of Eden—that if we disobey God we can then go on to be his equals.[4] We argue with God; we choose to revise his words and his will whenever these things don't coincide with our wishes. We know the reality is that we are part of God's creation and not ourselves the Creator. Yet we still persist in thinking we are God's equals. This is both stupid and irrational.

This wrong and foolish attitude needs to be repented of, if ever we are to relate to God as we ought.

Holiness as purity

We turn now to consider a second aspect of God's holiness, and that is his moral purity.

God is without sin; evil forms no part of his character. This truth about God's holiness is well described by the prophet Habakkuk. Habakkuk, chapter 1, says:

> You who are of purer eyes than to see evil
> and cannot look at wrong,

4 Genesis 3:5

> why do you idly look at traitors
> and are silent when the wicked swallows up
> the man more righteous than he? (Hab 1:13)

Notice that although Habakkuk is complaining bitterly, he simply takes it for granted that, of course, God is too pure to look on evil. This statement is so foundational and obvious to Habakkuk that he cannot see that it requires any proof at all. On this perfectly true assumption, he is then able to call upon God to do something to defeat evil, especially when it touches and affects the people of God.

This aspect of God's holiness is also illustrated in God's calling of the prophet Isaiah. Isaiah writes, in chapter 6:

> In the year that King Uzziah died I saw the Lord sitting upon a throne, high and lifted up; and the train of his robe filled the temple. Above him stood the seraphim. Each had six wings: with two he covered his face, and with two he covered his feet, and with two he flew. And one called to another and said:
>
> > "Holy, holy, holy is the LORD of hosts;
> > the whole earth is full of his glory!"
>
> And the foundations of the thresholds shook at the voice of him who called, and the house was filled with smoke. (Isa 6:1-4)

This is a vision of God in his inexpressible greatness and glory. See how Isaiah now responds to this terrifying vision of God in his majesty:

> And I said: "Woe is me! For I am lost; for I am a man of unclean lips, and I dwell in the midst of a people of unclean lips; for my eyes have seen the King, the LORD of hosts!" (Isa 6:5)

It has come home to Isaiah with great horror that he is sinful and God is pure. He cannot have relationship with God, unless first something fundamental changes. He is too tainted by sin and impurity to do anything else but wail in sheer terror. We remember God's word to Moses: "You cannot see my face, for man shall not see me and live" (Ex 33:20).

What changes? Isaiah is helpless to act. We read on and see that it is God himself who takes action through one of his spiritual servants:

> Then one of the seraphim flew to me, having in his hand a burning coal that he had taken with tongs from the altar. And he touched my mouth and said: "Behold, this has touched your lips; your guilt is taken away, and your sin atoned for". (Isa 6:6-7)

God is holy in the moral purity of his character: so perfectly holy that those who meet him must first have their sins dealt with.

We see this holiness of character once again in Luke, chapter 5:

> On one occasion, while the crowd was pressing in on him to hear the word of God, he was standing by the lake of Gennesaret, and he saw two boats by the lake, but the fishermen had gone out of them and were washing their nets. Getting into one of the boats, which was Simon's, he asked him to put out a little from the land. And he sat down and taught the people from the boat. And when he had finished speaking, he said to Simon, "Put out into the deep and let down your nets for a catch". And Simon answered, "Master, we toiled all night and took nothing! But at your word I will let down the nets." And when they had done this, they enclosed a large number of fish, and their nets were breaking. They signalled to their partners in the other boat to come and help them. And they came and filled both the boats, so that they began to sink. But when Simon Peter saw it, he fell down at Jesus' knees, saying, "Depart from me, for I am a sinful man, O Lord". For he and all who were with him were astonished at the catch of fish that they had taken, and so also were James and John, sons of Zebedee, who were partners with Simon. And Jesus said to Simon, "Do not be afraid; from now on you will be catching men". And when they had brought their boats to land, they left everything and followed him. (Luke 5:1-11)

Peter is overwhelmed with the greatness of the Lord Jesus. It is as if he reasoned, "If he knows all about the lake and everything in it, what then does he know about me?" He becomes dimly aware of his own sinfulness. Like Isaiah he is overtaken by the horror of this thought and he confesses his unworthiness. Like Isaiah, he understands that when he comes face-to-face with God, his sin must immediately be dealt with.

Similarly, when the apostle Paul encounters the risen Lord Jesus on the Damascus Road, he becomes aware of the depth of his rebellion against God. See how he recalls the incident when he describes it in Acts, chapter 26. Paul is addressing King Agrippa:

> "In this connection I journeyed to Damascus with the authority and commission of the chief priests. At midday, O king, I saw on the way a light from heaven, brighter than the sun, that shone around me and those who journeyed with me. And when we had all fallen to the ground, I heard a voice saying to me in the Hebrew language, 'Saul, Saul, why are you persecuting me? It is hard for you to kick against the goads.' And I said, 'Who are you, Lord?' And the Lord said, 'I am Jesus whom you are persecuting. But rise and stand upon your feet, for I have appeared to you for this purpose, to appoint you as a servant and witness to the things in which you have seen me and to those in which I will appear to you, delivering you from your people and from the Gentiles—to whom I am sending you to open their eyes, so that they may turn from darkness to light and from the power of Satan to God, that they may receive forgiveness of sins and a place among those who are sanctified by faith in me.'" (Acts 26:12-18)

What a terrible shock! Before this encounter, Saul (later named Paul, the Apostle) was so convinced that the Christians were mistaken that he did everything in his power to crush and destroy them. Then the risen Christ confronted him. The encounter was so literally awe-full that he and his companions fell to the ground, unable to continue in their quest. At that very moment, Paul saw and understood that the whole direction of his life had been in complete error. Something had to be done; his sin and rebellion had to be dealt with, and the direction of his life now had to go through a 180-degree change.

We meet a final example in the book of Revelation. Here, we are given a description of the risen Lord Jesus and his appearing to the Apostle John. In Revelation, chapter 1, John writes:

> I, John, your brother and partner in the tribulation and the kingdom and the patient endurance that are in Jesus, was on the island called Patmos on account of the word of God and the testimony of Jesus. I was in the Spirit on the Lord's day, and I heard behind me a loud voice like a trumpet saying, "Write what you see in a book and send it to the seven churches, to Ephesus and to Smyrna and to Pergamum and to Thyatira and to Sardis and to Philadelphia and to Laodicea."

> Then I turned to see the voice that was speaking to me, and on turning I saw seven golden lampstands, and in the midst of the lampstands one like a son of man, clothed with a long robe and with a golden sash around his chest. The hairs of his head were white like wool, as white as snow. His eyes were like a flame of fire, his feet were like burnished bronze, refined in a furnace, and his voice was like the roar of many waters. In his right hand he held seven stars, from his mouth came a sharp two-edged sword, and his face was like the sun shining in full strength. (Rev 1:9-16)

John reacts to the revealing of Jesus' glory and holiness in a way with which we are now familiar.

> When I saw him, I fell at his feet as though dead. But he laid his right hand on me, saying, "Fear not, I am the first and the last, and the living one. I died, and behold I am alive forevermore, and I have the keys of Death and Hades." (Rev 1:17-18)

Each time the people involved in these encounters react, it is with an awareness of their own sinfulness, and with repentance. This is as it should be, and the response of repentance immediately brings comfort and reassurance from God who is as gracious and compassionate as he is holy.

We are not like God

Once we see God as he really is, we find that we are not like him. We cannot match him in strength and power, nor are we pure in heart like him.

What's more, we also discover that we are, at least in part, morally guilty for our failure to be like God in his holiness. Of course, in the matter of power and strength, we lack his holiness because we are his creatures; we are not the Creator. But in the other aspect of holiness, that is, purity of heart—well we lack this because of sinful decisions that we have made, and the awful consequences that follow from early bad choices.

The reality of our situation in the face of God's holiness is that we have turned our backs on him. We've pretended that we are his equals. We've argued with him and we've ignored him. This is what the Bible means when it says that we are 'sinful'. Instead of reflecting the image of our Creator, we have attempted to remake him in our image. Recognizing this error in ourselves is a basic and necessary step towards true holiness.

God's plan for us

God's plan for us is that we should be holy in character as he is holy in character. The following verses illustrate this clearly:

> For [our fathers] disciplined us for a short time as it seemed best to them, but he disciplines us for our good, that we may share his holiness. (Heb 12:10)

> For this is the will of God, your sanctification[5] ... (1 Thess 4:3)

> And we know that for those who love God all things work together for good, for those who are called according to his purpose. For those whom he foreknew he also predestined to be conformed to the image of his Son, in order that he might be the firstborn among many brothers. And those whom he predestined he also called, and those whom he called he also justified, and those whom he justified he also glorified. (Rom 8:28-30)

God's plan is that we will be holy, that all the Christlike characteristics will be formed in us. In fact, this is what life is about. The more I grow like Jesus, the more successful I am. The less like Jesus I am, the more I have failed in life. It has little to do with how much money I make, what my career is, how the family is. In the end the real thing in life is "are we holy as God is holy?"

It was quite a while in the Christian life before I realized this. I had my Christian life in one box closed up

5 The words 'sanctification', 'sanctified' and 'holy', together with the word 'saint', are all taken from the one Greek word in the original language of the New Testament.

tightly and the rest of my life in another. I thought I would be a successful Christian if I was successful in my career. In fact I believed that the more successful my career, the more I was living the Christian life the way God wanted it. It didn't occur to me to ask the question, "What would Christ do in this situation?" or even, "What does the Bible say?" I just pressed on with what I thought would make me a success. This is quite different to the Bible's understanding of living the holy life.

Holiness begins with repentance and faith

The only wise and intelligent response for humans encountering the holy God is repentance and faith.[6] Indeed, this is the way we begin the Christian life. The apostle Paul holds up as a model for all Christians to follow the way the Thessalonians responded to the gospel. This is how he describes it:

> For they themselves report concerning us the kind of reception we had among you, and how you turned to God from idols to serve the living and true God, and to wait for his Son from heaven, whom he raised from the dead, Jesus who delivers us from the wrath to come. (1 Thess 1:9-10)

6 Acts 20:21

What is repentance?

Let us begin to clear away some of the dead wood from our thinking by being clear, firstly, about what repentance is *not*.

Repentance is *not*, at its core, simply a sense of sorrow—feeling sorry for something. Sorrow may *accompany* true repentance, but it is not the essence of it. A person may be genuinely repentant and yet not feel much sorrow at all, or indeed any deep emotion. On the other hand, it is possible to be full of sorrow and sadness, but not to have made a single step towards repentance.[7] The person might simply feel sorrow over having been found out in a compromising situation!

Repentance must be understood, rather, as a complete change in direction. It is an about-face with regard to God, and with regard to the way we relate to him. In the past we may have ignored, disobeyed and even argued with God. Now, however, the repentant person has turned away from this behaviour and has decided to serve God in a way which is pleasing to him instead.

Did you notice how the Thessalonians responded? They "turned to God from idols to serve the living and true God". They may well have previously worshipped the Greek or Roman gods. At heart, it is fair to assume that they were worshippers of themselves, simply projecting their desires and fears on to invented gods. That behaviour stopped, however, when they repented.

7 Hebrews 12:17

They rejected this former way of life and said, "From this day onward, I am serving the living and true God".

Repentance is well illustrated by the story the Lord Jesus tells in Matthew:

> "What do you think? A man had two sons. And he went to the first and said, 'Son, go and work in the vineyard today'. And he answered, 'I will not', but afterward he changed his mind and went. And he went to the other son and said the same. And he answered, 'I go, sir', but did not go. Which of the two did the will of his father?" They said, "The first". Jesus said to them, "Truly, I say to you, the tax collectors and the prostitutes go into the kingdom of God before you. For John came to you in the way of righteousness, and you did not believe him, but the tax collectors and the prostitutes believed him. And even when you saw it, you did not afterward change your minds and believe him." (Matt 21:28-32)

Did you notice that the first son's initial response was "I will not go and work in the vineyard today"? However, he changed his mind and went. He, in fact, repented.

May I ask you if you have done that?

It would be foolish to think that you could have a life of holiness and yet not have begun correctly. Now would be a wonderful time to begin, if you have not already done so. Why not stop reading for a moment and tell God that you wish to change your behaviour towards him and that, from today on, you will serve him as the true and living God?

Not only repentance, but faith as well

Repentance, however, is not enough! Let us look again at the example of the Thessalonians:

> ... and to wait for his Son from heaven, whom he raised from the dead, Jesus who delivers us from the wrath to come. (1 Thess 1:10)

They not only repented, but they also transferred their trust[8] from themselves and their idols, and instead placed their trust in the Lord Jesus to be their rescuer on the day of judgement.

No doubt Paul had told them they were sinners, in as much as they had not served God as their God, that this was a serious situation, and that, unless they repented, they would be lost on the future day of God's wrath.

No doubt Paul had also told them that Jesus had taken the punishment their sins deserved when he died on the cross for them, and that they could be completely forgiven if they put their trust in the promise that God would receive them on the merit of Jesus' death.

So their faith was firmly grounded in the facts of Jesus' life, death and resurrection.

Now the essential element of this faith *in Jesus*—the

8 In the original Greek of the New Testament, the words for 'faith', 'trust', and 'belief' are identical. They mean more than head knowledge; they refer to a complete and total reliance on the thing or person that is trusted.

faith that the Thessalonians had, and that we must also have—is not simply a vague spiritual feeling of some sort. The essential element of faith is not even how *much* of this trust that someone has. The essential element of faith in Jesus is that such faith is *in Jesus*; not in ourselves, not in anyone or anything else. This essential element is what actually makes faith effective, useful and attractive. If our faith is not *in Jesus*, then it is no different from the faith that any other person might have in money, success, family or achievement.

True faith, then, is when I stop trusting in myself and my own goodness, and transfer my trust to the God who promises to forgive me because of the death of Jesus.

Such faith is well illustrated in Romans 4. Abraham is held up for us as a man of faith. See how his faith is described:

> No distrust made him waver concerning the promise of God, but he grew strong in his faith as he gave glory to God, fully convinced that God was able to do what he had promised. (Rom 4:20-21)

He was fully persuaded that God had power to keep his promise.

Are you fully persuaded that God will forgive and receive you on the basis that Christ's death is sufficient to cleanse you from every sin?[9]

9 1 John 1:7

Why not tell God that you agree that you need forgiveness and ask him to forgive you and enable you to put your trust in the death of Jesus?

To summarize the point that is being made here: a life of holiness begins with repentance and faith as the appropriate way of responding to the holiness of God.

HOLINESS

2. How it progresses

PEOPLE SEEM READY TO stick all sorts of odd messages on the back of their cars:

My other car is a Rolls Royce

Baby on board

Remember to breathe

One day I came across a car and on the back window it had the sign “Honk if you love Jesus”. It seemed like quite an extraordinary response to ask for, but since it seemed important to the driver, I obliged. I honked loudly. The driver looked daggers at me in the rear vision mirror. As he appeared to have misunderstood, I gave him a ‘one-way-Jesus’ hand signal. I was surprised when he gave me an extremely vulgar hand signal back. His response seemed most odd. It occurred to me that perhaps he had borrowed his son’s car for the afternoon.

On another occasion I read the sign “Christians are

not perfect, just forgiven". While I agree with this statement, it is not really the full picture of what the Christian life is about. Christians are forgiven people, that is true. But we must also insist that they are people who are now pressing on to Christlikeness of character. It would be *equally* true to say that Christians are not yet perfect, but that is the direction in which they are heading.

Is perfection in Christ your goal in life?

In the previous chapter, I made the point that holiness begins with repentance and faith. Not only does holiness begin with repentance and faith, it also proceeds with repentance and faith. That is why we never grow out of the gospel, which leads us always to the same response—repentance and faith. The gospel of Jesus Christ is as good and important and relevant today as it was on the first day that we heard it and embraced it as true. We come to Christ by the gospel, we stay in Christ by the gospel, we die in Christ by the gospel, and in glory we will sing the gospel song, such as the song of Moses and the Lamb in Revelation 15:3-4 that John heard sung by the saints in heaven.

If we have grown tired of hearing that gospel of grace, it is because either we are unconverted or what is being preached to us is not the gospel.

I remember reading about a young man who approached the Pictures Editor of the *Sydney Morning Herald* and asked for a job as a photographer. The Pictures Editor asked a stock question: "What is your aim in life?" The boy thought for a while and said, "To know, love and serve my God". I don't know if this is anything like what the Editor was expecting. He may have been wanting to hear something along the lines of "To be the best photographer in the world". I haven't met any Pictures Editors lately, but I know I would as soon have answered to one of Nero's pet lions as to have said what the young photographer said.

And yet, what a wonderful answer! "To know, love and serve my God."

In this chapter, I want us to consider in some detail the following passage from Hebrews 12:

> For [our fathers] disciplined us for a short time as it seemed best to them, but he disciplines us for our good, *that we may share his holiness*. For the moment all discipline seems painful rather than pleasant, but later it yields the peaceful fruit of righteousness to those who have been trained by it. (Heb 12:10-11, my italics)

God's plan for us is clearly stated here: "That we may share his holiness".

In Romans 8, we read the same idea although stated differently:

> And we know that for those who love God all things work together for good, for those who are called according to his purpose. For those whom he foreknew he also predestined *to be conformed to the image of his Son*, in order that he might be the firstborn among many brothers. And those whom

> he predestined he also called, and those whom he called he also justified, and those whom he justified he also glorified. (Romans 8:28-30, my italics)

God's plan for us is "to be conformed to the image of his Son". Titus 2 expresses the same idea this way:

> For the grace of God has appeared, bringing salvation for all people, training us to renounce ungodliness and worldly passions, and to live self-controlled, upright, and godly lives in the present age, waiting for our blessed hope, the appearing of the glory of our great God and Savior Jesus Christ, who gave himself for us to redeem us from all lawlessness and to purify for himself a people for his own possession who are zealous for good works. (Titus 2:11-14)

The end or purpose of God's gracious salvation is to purify a new people for himself who are "zealous for good works".

To sum up these ideas, we can see that God's plan for us is Christlikeness of character, and that we make progress in the Christian life by pressing on to the end.

Self-discipline and God's discipline

In Hebrews 12, the method for obtaining holiness is self-discipline and God's discipline.

Most Christians are looking for holiness and some wish that God would give it to them like a pill. We could take it and 'Hey Presto!' we would be immediately holy. It sounds like a wonderful idea, but the reality just doesn't work that way. In Hebrews 12, living the Christian life is likened to running a race:

> Therefore, since we are surrounded by so great a cloud of witnesses, let us also lay aside every weight, and sin which clings so closely, and let us run with endurance the race that is set before us, looking to Jesus, the founder and perfecter of our faith, who for the joy that was set before him endured the cross, despising the shame, and is seated at the right hand of the throne of God.
>
> Consider him who endured from sinners such hostility against himself, so that you may not grow weary or fainthearted. (Heb 12:1-3)

Before we look at this passage in detail it might be helpful to be reminded about the background of the letter to the Hebrews. This letter was directed to Jewish Christians. They had been converted to Christ. Life for them since then had been extremely difficult and painful. They were tempted to drift back into Judaism. Perhaps they asked themselves, "Why, if I am God's person, is life so hard and strenuous?" It is likely that when they went to church, church was small and didn't seem nearly as grand as taking a sacrifice to the temple. Possibly they were undergoing physical persecution or ostracism from friends and family. We can't be exactly sure what the cause of their difficulty was, but we do know that they were about to drift back to where they were before they came to Christ.

In response, the writer of Hebrews warns them that there is nothing further in Judaism now that Christ has come and died and risen for them. Hard and all as it was to resist persecution, the writer urges them to follow the men and women of faith who did not give up, whatever the cost. Indeed, some who had gone before had even forfeited their lives rather than give up. These men and women are the great crowd of witnesses he is referring to here in Hebrews 12.

Self-discipline

1. Throw off everything that hinders

It is interesting to see that the writer does not say whether the things to be thrown off are good or bad. They could well have been very *good* things or activities that they were now being called upon to give up. For another person, or at a different time, it could be a legitimate thing or activity. However, the principle that is being explained in these verses is this: if at any time or in any circumstance the thing or activity gets in the way of growing like Christ, it is at that time or in that circumstance to be discarded.

When I travel overseas, I have never yet found a way to cut down on my luggage. Friends of mine can go for months with just a change of underwear and a spare shirt, which they then wash as they go. That is not me. I carry away and bring home clothes that I have never even put on. Generally, the overcoat I wear is stuffed with hankies and underwear to disguise the true weight of my carry-on luggage!

Our writer is saying something like this: "You cannot run in a race if you wear your overcoat and especially if the pockets are stuffed full. You might make it in a short dash, but the Christian life is a marathon."

He is calling on us to be rigorous in self-examination, and to understand that growing Christlike is so important that we should not let anything hinder it. It is possible to be hindered by some thing, which, even though it is not sinful within itself, nevertheless gets in the way of holiness. As you read this, you may be reminded of some thing that is good, but which really robs you of the best. You may be conscious that you have *chosen* this good thing, rather than the best thing. If this is so, then throw it away. It could be the way you use money. It might be the way you use time. It may be the way you use your talents and abilities.

There is nothing wrong with spending a weekend at the snow. However, if it means leaving your Sunday School class without a teacher on Sunday, then you don't have to be a genius to know whether the good (going to the snow) has robbed you of the best (teaching your Sunday School class). Now it is possible to be sufficiently far-sighted to see that if you take on the task of teaching Sunday School you will never be able to have a weekend at the snow. To choose not to do Sunday School teaching *for this reason* is to stuff the overcoat with everything you own.

If you have been taught, like most people, that you should maximize your potential and be the very best you can, here is a thought worth pondering: it is simply not possible for us who are "made in the image of God" ever to reach our full potential in this life! There are too many things that we could be good at. What is more, we were made for eternity. There is not enough time now to do everything. Because in this life we will certainly run out of time, we are forced to make choices that we would never have to make if we lived forever.

So we see that God, in this part of the Bible, is urging us to throw away everything which hinders us from *following Christ* to the best of our ability. Whether or not the thought consoles us (and it ought to), it is true to say that in eternity there will be time to do every single thing that there wasn't time to do in the here and now.

2. Throw off the sin which so easily entangles

We must put sin behind us. By this, the writer means the sinful issues which dog our footsteps every moment. We may have recognized the sin for what it is, we may have confessed it and we may have asked for forgiveness, but the step of saying to ourself, "This must come to an end. I renounce it", seems not to have happened. Our writer says to us, "Do it!" Now is the time to act.

He expects that we will be self-disciplined and ruthless towards sin. He is telling us to recognize it for what it is, and then to call on God to strengthen us so that we will rigorously fight against it and renounce it. Sin is to be seen for what it is, something that is totally incongruous with the Christian walk. It matters not at all how many times we may have failed in a particular matter in the past.

There is a story told about someone who has been bugged by a persistent sin. He had given in to temptation yet again, and in his prayers he confessed his sin by saying, "Oh God, I've done it again", to which God replied, "Done what?"

God completely forgives us, and we should believe him and act accordingly.

3. Run the race with perseverance

'The race' we are running is no short dash. It is a day-in, day-out marathon of enormous proportions. For myself, I have been running this race for more than 50 years. No doubt this is why I am told to do it with patience and perseverance! It requires continual hard work, effort and energy. The final prize, however, is worth every moment of agony and strain.

Recently a friend of mine was watching the Olympic Games on the television with his children. One of them expressed the idea that she would love to win an event at an Olympic Games and be awarded a gold medal. All the other children agreed immediately. They wanted to do it, too. "Well," said my friend, "that is an excellent idea. And now, while you are still young, would be the ideal time to start training." This suggestion was met with a great deal of enthusiasm. Before the afternoon came to an end, they had all decided to enrol in a programme the following Saturday, and then to spend each of their subsequent Saturday mornings training hard at 'Little Athletics'. As Saturday approached, so their level of excitement grew.

Unfortunately, their happiness and anticipation evaporated like the morning dew when they were sent to run around the oval. But this was not the only exercise that they were required to perform. They spent the entire morning going from one strenuous exercise to another and, as if that wasn't enough, they also finished with another run around the oval.

It was very difficult to raise enough enthusiasm to go the following Saturday. After Little Athletics had finished that day, they announced they didn't really want to win a gold medal after all. "Well", announced their father, "we have paid for the term and we will continue for the rest of the term". From the Wednesday of each week, like clockwork, they would start to get 'sick' and plead the absolute impossibility of going to Little Athletics that Saturday.

In growing and becoming like Christ, each of us wants to win a gold medal. But the hard yards of training Little Athletics-style week-in and week-out can frequently lack appeal.

However, keeping our eyes on the goal will help a great deal.

4. Fix our eyes on Jesus, the author and perfecter of our faith

> [Let us look] to Jesus, the founder and perfecter of our faith, who for the joy that was set before him endured the cross, despising the shame, and is seated at the right hand of the throne of God.
>
> Consider him who endured from sinners such hostility against himself, so that you may not grow weary or fainthearted. (Heb 12:2-3)

The end product of casting off and running the race with patience is that we will share in the glory of the Lord Jesus Christ. The writer reminds us of Jesus' perseverance for us. He did not give up. Imagine if Jesus in the Garden of Gethsemane had said something like, "It really is too hard. I've done enough. I'm going back to heaven." The notion is simply unthinkable.

Jesus did not give up until his work of sin-bearing on the cross was achieved, at which point he was able to say, "It is finished" (John 19:30). He did not grow weary. He did not lose heart in any way. He ran the course that was set before him, and so obtained a salvation for his people. If he had failed and given in, we would not have been saved. The "joy" that was "set before him" was the salvation of the world.

In the 'race' of Christlikeness of character, we are to keep our eyes set on the goal so that we will not grow weary and not lose heart. Be assured that one day we will be exactly like the Lord Jesus. Don't give up and don't give in to the idea that it is too hard. It is not too hard when you think of the great blessing that is in store for you.

On several occasions during my Christian life, I have been offered quick fix methods of obtaining holiness without the hard work of self-discipline. Some told me I would obtain it by a method of absolute surrender. Others suggested that I might need to be baptised with the Holy Spirit, after which the Christian life would grow ever easier. Still others told of continuous victory over all my sins, and how I could have that if I asked for it. They all turned out to be waterless springs, promising things that they were unable to deliver. They offered me heaven (which was irresistible) and the assurance that it would happen now (which was impossible). Every method offered required no effort on my part. Our writer would have considered these various methods and said, "It is not possible".

If it all depended on us, however, we might easily grow discouraged. But it doesn't all depend on us. From a heavenly perspective, our present difficulties may be understood as God's disciplining of us to become more and more like Christ.

God's discipline

So that we will not be totally discouraged, we are reminded in Hebrews 12 that God is at work with us

and that he will not give up.

> In your struggle against sin you have not yet resisted to the point of shedding your blood. And have you forgotten the exhortation that addresses you as sons?
>
> "My son, do not regard lightly the discipline of
> the Lord,
> nor be weary when reproved by him.
> For the Lord disciplines the one he loves,
> and chastises every son whom he receives."
>
> It is for discipline that you have to endure. God is treating you as sons. For what son is there whom his father does not discipline? If you are left without discipline, in which all have participated, then you are illegitimate children and not sons. Besides this, we have had earthly fathers who disciplined us and we respected them. Shall we not much more be subject to the Father of spirits and live? For they disciplined us for a short time as it seemed best to them, but he disciplines us for our good, that we may share his holiness. For the moment all discipline seems painful rather than pleasant, but later it yields the peaceful fruit of righteousness to those who have been trained by it.
>
> Therefore lift your drooping hands and strengthen your weak knees, and make straight paths for your feet, so that what is lame may not be put out of joint but rather be healed. (Heb 12:4-13)

What this part of God's word is saying at first seems

very odd. To begin with, the writer says words to this effect: "You are alive. It might be difficult, but it hasn't been fatal."

This may seem like a very weak form of encouragement indeed. But in speaking in this way, the writer is helping us by forcing us to think about the reason *why* God might bring such difficulty upon us. His answer is to point out that the suffering is not accidental in any way. Rather, God's hand of discipline is to mould us because we are his heirs and have a great inheritance to receive. And why would God take so much trouble to see that we grow Christlike? It is simply because he loves us. He has his eye not only on present suffering, but also on who we will become. It is because we are true children that he acts in a fatherly way towards us.

This is also the wonderful promise of Romans 8:28-30—that God works in all things to conform us to the image of his Son, and that he will make sure that the process finally comes to completion.

The verses we read in Hebrews 12 tell us that God will not give up. He will work away on us, and will *continue* to work away on us until he has completed his work. I find that very reassuring. I hope you do too. This being the case, it will be far better and wiser if we don't resist God's will but work towards the same goal.

There is no question that from time to time, we will find that this process is plain hard work. You may be the only Christian at your workplace. Following Jesus by being an honest, diligent worker is extremely difficult. You may be the only Christian in your family, and they all think you are odd. You may wonder if it is worth the effort to try to keep on being pure in your thinking, or truthful in speech, or trustworthy in keeping promises. You may be tempted to say, "It is just too hard". The Bible's reassurance and instruction is simple: Don't give in. It should reassure you that you really *are* a child of God and to know that he is preparing you for a great inheritance. You may be out of work, you may have lost your boyfriend or your girlfriend, or you may just be growing old. You may be tempted in the middle of all this to imagine that God doesn't care. Nothing could be further from the truth. It is the exact opposite: God cares for us more than anyone and will continue to protect us, work in us, and discipline us as his true children.

Please note verse 11: "For the moment all discipline seems painful rather than pleasant, but later it yields the peaceful fruit of righteousness to those who have been trained by it". What does this process yield? It yields righteousness and peace.

It is so that we will share in his holiness.

Did you notice in Hebrews 12 how often the idea of struggling comes in?[10] Therefore, please do not listen to people who say they have a quick-fix method to reach holiness.

10 Verses 1, 4, 7, 12 and 14.

A second exhortation to holiness

> Therefore lift your drooping hands and strengthen your weak knees, and make straight paths for your feet, so that what is lame may not be put out of joint but rather be healed. (Heb 12:12-13)

The metaphor in verse 13 calls us to do some repairs to the pathway along which we are all walking. The idea is that if it is rough and uneven, the lame person will fall over. So what is the reality behind the metaphor? The following verses explain this, and also act as a commentary about self-discipline.

> Strive for peace with everyone, and for the holiness without which no one will see the Lord. (Heb 12:14)

The New Testament in many places calls us to make every effort to be at peace with each other.[11] There would be no need to do this if we were not selfish people. It is a matter to be worked at.

> See to it that no one fails to obtain the grace of God; that no "root of bitterness" springs up and causes trouble, and by it many become defiled. (Heb 12:15)

Here the writer seems to be asking us to take care of the other Christians around us. If we see or hear of Christians who are about to drift away from God, we are to take action to restore them. The reference to the

11 Romans 12:18, Titus 2:9-10.

"root of bitterness" is a reference to Deuteronomy 29:18 where Moses is warning the children of Israel to not even think about idolatry or envy those who worship idols so that a bitter root will not spring up within them and cause them to go after it.

Have you noticed as you read the book of Numbers how every time the journey through the desert becomes difficult the people grumble against God and say, "We should never have left Egypt". The people of Israel looked back and envied others, and after a while they wanted to be like them. It was almost as if they had forgotten completely the terrible slavery they had experienced while living in Egypt. Do you recall how God described it when he was speaking to Moses at the burning bush?

> Then the LORD said, "I have surely seen the affliction of my people who are in Egypt and have heard their cry because of their taskmasters. I know their sufferings, and I have come down to deliver them out of the hand of the Egyptians and to bring them up out of that land to a good and broad land, a land flowing with milk and honey ...". (Exod 3:7-8)

Do you think it is possible for us to become discouraged in a similar way? What would it look like for us? We may say to ourselves, "It was easier when I wasn't a Christian. I didn't worry then about sin, but now it is so hard to fight at every step of the way."

A part of our problem here may be that we have

forgotten what it was like, before we came to Christ. And what was it like? Our sins were unforgiven. We were certainly on our way to hell. We knew nothing of the Holy Spirit's presence guiding us and assuring us that we really are God's children.

You may know someone who is like that. Our writer is saying that we should be helping them.

> [See] that no one is sexually immoral or unholy like Esau, who sold his birthright for a single meal. For you know that afterward, when he desired to inherit the blessing, he was rejected, for he found no chance to repent, though he sought it with tears. (Heb 12:16-17)

Perhaps the thought of the pagan temples and worship has sparked the writer's mind to think about sexual sins. They were often associated together. He may just have thought that it was a possible area where Christians too could slip up in our relationships with each other. If this is a present problem for you, then quickly repent and help others to do so too.

His last exhortation is not to be 'godless' or profane. Esau is used as an example. Esau was the eldest of the twins born to Isaac and Rebekah. As the first-born he would inherit the largest part of his father's inheritance and as well he would inherit the spiritual oversight of their clan. He would be their shepherd, under God. He was to be the leader of the people of God. This was a great responsibility and privilege.

Jacob, Esau's twin brother, was envious of this blessing. He bargained with Esau to swap his birthright for a meal. Esau was famished at the time, but he valued spiritual matters so little that his birthright seemed like nothing, so he exchanged it.[12] Many years later, he realized what a foolish thing he had done and he longed to get it back. He had so hardened his heart against the things of God, however, that he could find no room in his heart for repentance.

God, in the book of Hebrews, is urging us to keep looking at Jesus and not to the world around us.

Don't think about life like the pagans do.[13] We must not envy them or we will want to return to our former godless ways. God is calling on us to think about the goal to which we are heading and not only to think about the present. If Esau had thought about the future, he would not have despised his birthright.

Remember: "Strive for peace with everyone, and for the holiness without which no one will see the Lord" (Heb 12:14).

12 Genesis 25:27ff

13 Cf. Matthew 6:31-33

HOLINESS

3. Its fulfilment

TRY TO IMAGINE this wedding.

The groom has been up since the crack of dawn. He is scrubbed clean. He has tried several aftershave lotions and has washed each successive one off. He is wearing a suit, which is a special concession to his future mother-in-law. His shirt has odd frills down the front and at the cuffs, and he wears a bow tie. The best man and his groomsman are similarly dressed. His mates have already had a dig at him. Most people think he looks quite handsome, but he feels like a total idiot. For the sake of his bride he has dressed himself up, and now he is determined to see it through.

He and the boys are now in the church, and as the wedding march sounds from the organ, he looks around to discover his bride is in an old tracksuit. She is having the classic bad hair day, and she looks as if she has been greasing the car.

This may not be a bad scenario for a B-grade romantic comedy, but the idea of this actually happening in real life is beyond imagination!

At every wedding I have either attended or witnessed through photographs or videos, the bride has made every effort to present herself as beautifully as it is possible to present herself. It is always apparent that great time and effort have been expended in order to bring about the hoped-for result. The process of getting ready will have begun long before, with plans for the wedding day and wedding dress made in painstaking detail. Every stage of the process will have been thought through and considered. Most likely, the last minute efforts to keep those plans on track will have commenced early on the day of the wedding. For such an occasion, there is simply no question that the bride will be at her best.

Holiness reaches *its* fulfilment in a wonderful picture of Christ's bride beautifully adorned for her husband on her wedding day. You and I, and every Christian person, will share in this wonderful event.

> Then I saw a new heaven and a new earth, for the first heaven and the first earth had passed away, and the sea was no more. And I saw the holy city, new Jerusalem, coming down out of heaven from God, prepared as a bride adorned for her husband. And I heard a loud voice from the throne saying, "Behold, the dwelling place of God is with man. He will

> dwell with them, and they will be his people, and God himself will be with them as their God. He will wipe away every tear from their eyes, and death shall be no more, neither shall there be mourning nor crying nor pain anymore, for the former things have passed away."
>
> And he who was seated on the throne said, "Behold, I am making all things new." (Rev 21:1-5)

Because we are not meant to turn up in our dirty old tracksuit with a smudge of grease on our cheeks and our hair like a bird's nest, God continues to transform us into the likeness of Christ, so we will be prepared for that day when we will take our place in the New Creation God is preparing for us.

Let us summarize at this point where we have come from in our consideration of the subject of holiness. Firstly, in Chapter 1 we have considered that holiness begins with God changing us into new people.[14] We respond with repentance and faith.

Next, in Chapter 2, we have considered that holiness proceeds with God making us into Christlike people. See what God says in 2 Corinthians 3:

> And we all, with unveiled face, beholding the glory of the Lord, are being transformed into the same image from one degree of glory to another. For this comes from the Lord who is the Spirit. (2 Cor 3:18)

14 2 Corinthians 5:21

"The glory of the Lord" is revealed in the person of Jesus and in Jesus' work. We see this principally in the gospel. We gaze on his glory by reading about him and thinking about him in the gospel. As we do this, the Holy Spirit changes us into his glory.

Charles Wesley expresses it beautifully in his hymn:

> Changed from glory into glory,
> Till in heaven we take our place,
> Til we cast our crowns before thee,
> Lost in wonder, love and praise![15]

It is a very great work, and it continues for an entire lifetime of a Christian.

Thirdly and finally, we now consider that holiness will have reached its fulfilment when we take our place in the New Creation.

> But according to his promise we are waiting for new heavens and a new earth in which righteousness dwells. (2 Pet 3:13)

Did you notice how the new heaven and earth is described? It's the place "in which righteousness dwells". That is why we are getting in practice at the present moment. We don't want to arrive at this glorious scene and discover that everyone is wearing a dinner jacket while we are wearing our shorts.

15 Charles Wesley (1707-88), *Love Divine All Loves Excelling*

In this chapter, let us consider more carefully the question, "Where does holiness reach its fulfilment?"

It is extremely important to keep looking to the end. The Christian life is difficult, and if we lose this perspective it may prove too difficult.

So let us return to Hebrews, chapter 12:

> For you have not come to what may be touched, a blazing fire and darkness and gloom and a tempest and the sound of a trumpet and a voice whose words made the hearers beg that no further messages be spoken to them. For they could not endure the order that was given, "If even a beast touches the mountain, it shall be stoned". Indeed, so terrifying was the sight that Moses said, "I tremble with fear". (Heb 12:18-21)

What is being described here is Moses at Mt Sinai where the Law was given.[16] It was awesome. To be in the presence of the living God shocked even Moses. Even though this appearance was temporary for the purpose of giving the Law, it was nonetheless terrifying. The idea that the living God was speaking was astonishing. However our writer says that our experience is different.

> But you have come to Mount Zion and to the city of the living God, the heavenly Jerusalem, and to

16 Exodus 19

> innumerable angels in festal gathering, and to the assembly of the firstborn who are enrolled in heaven, and to God, the judge of all, and to the spirits of the righteous made perfect, and to Jesus, the mediator of a new covenant, and to the sprinkled blood that speaks a better word than the blood of Abel. (Heb 12:22-24)

We have arrived at something that is much bigger in every way. We have arrived at Mt Zion, the heavenly Jerusalem. We have arrived at a permanent presence of God with his people. Because we are in Christ, we have already arrived where he is. We know this now by faith, but the time will come when we will know it because we will see it.

It is because of this that we are warned to take care now how we hear the word of God. Awesome as it was at Sinai, it should not be less full of awe to us now that we have been forgiven and made children of God. We, if it were possible, should be more terrified not to listen and obey the God who speaks.

> See to it that you do not refuse him who is speaking. (Heb 12:25)

God came briefly at Sinai to give the Law, but we have arrived at the mountain of God where we can see the full effect of the gospel, permanently. We should be eager to hear the voice of God and to obey him. It is as if our writer is saying to us, “Take care. Do not refuse him who is speaking.”

I have already told you I have been a Christian for a long time. I don't know how many sermons I have heard over the years. I guess it would be thousands (not counting the ones I have preached!). It's quite possible that you too, as the reader of this book, will have heard hundreds or even thousands of sermons in your time as a Christian. Do you think in those circumstances it is possible that we can become dull to the wonder of what is taking place? Have we grown used to the wonder that God is speaking to his people?

The high moment of our gathering should be when the Bible is read and when the Scriptures are being explained. Do we consider that we are people who stand in awe of the living God speaking? We should go to church, week by week, with a heart full of expectancy, longing to hear the voice of God. We should be people who can be relied upon to be at prayer for the preacher and to encourage him. Indeed, we should be regularly at prayer that God will raise up more and more competent preachers of his word, begging him not to leave us without teachers who love and honour him and his word.

Even as you are reading this now, why not stop and pray for your minister and his preaching! Pray for yourself, that you will be a good listener, someone who is quick to hear and quick to obey.

The great inevitability

Please look again at Hebrews 12:

> See that you do not refuse him who is speaking. For if they did not escape when they refused him who warned them on earth, much less will we escape if we reject him who warns from heaven. At that time his voice shook the earth, but now he has promised, "Yet once more I will shake not only the earth but also the heavens". This phrase, "Yet once more", indicates the removal of things that are shaken—that is, things that have been made—in order that the things that cannot be shaken may remain. (Heb 12:25-27)

There is in this passage a great inevitability, and a warning. The warning is to heed God's word.

The inevitability is the final judgement of God. The idea is this: if the Israelites did not escape when they ignored the word of God, spoken on earth (that is, from Mount Sinai), how ever will we escape if we neglect the word of God spoken from heaven (that is, the heavenly Jerusalem)? The writer then proceeds to tell us why we should pay attention to the word of God. His reason is that judgement will come and God will shake away everything that is not of lasting benefit. In verse 26, the writer quotes Haggai, the prophet.

Some background to this prophecy may help.

The people of God have been told that if they do not obey God and worship him exclusively, they will not be able to stay in the Promised Land. They persist in rebellion and they are therefore deported into Babylon. They stay there until 70 years elapse and then they are allowed home again. When the exiles return, they rebuild the walls and city of Jerusalem and the temple. Hardly any of them are old enough to remember the temple that Solomon built, but their fathers and their grandfathers had told them of its splendour. The new one, by comparison, was a great disappointment. It was neither big nor beautiful, and on the day of its consecration there was weeping as well as cheering. By way of encouraging the governor Zerubbabel, Haggai says this:

> In the seventh month, on the twenty-first day of the month, the word of the LORD came by the hand of Haggai the prophet, "Speak now to Zerubbabel the son of Shealtiel, governor of Judah, and to Joshua the son of Jehozadak, the high priest, and to all the remnant of the people, and say, 'Who is left among you who saw this house in its former glory? How do you see it now? Is it not as nothing in your eyes? Yet now be strong, O Zerubbabel, declares the LORD. Be strong, O Joshua, son of Jehozadak, the high priest. Be strong, all you people of the land, declares the LORD. Work, for I am with you, declares the LORD of hosts, according to the covenant that I made with you when you came out of Egypt. My Spirit remains in your midst. Fear not. For thus says the LORD of hosts: Yet once more, in a little while, I will shake the heavens and the earth and the sea and the dry land. And I will shake all

> nations, so that the treasures of all nations shall come in, and I will fill this house with glory, says the LORD of hosts. The silver is mine, and the gold is mine, declares the LORD of hosts. The latter glory of this house shall be greater than the former, says the LORD of hosts. And in this place I will give peace, declares the LORD of hosts.'" (Hag 2:1-9)

This word of encouragement is that God will do such a great thing that they will marvel at it. The writer to the Hebrews runs with this idea and says it refers to the final judgement. God will shake the universe and everything in it and he will shake out everything that is not good and wholesome.

If you have ever panned for gold (admittedly not a common activity these days) you will know that the process involves shovelling earth and stones into a pan, and then shaking the dirt, washing it and shaking it until only the nuggets of gold are left.

It is a similar idea here. God will shake the universe until only the good is left. It will be a purifying process. This is a very good reason to make sure that we are not 'shaken away' in this process. Did you notice that even the nations will be shaken? Nothing except the godly will be left. Only God's unshakable kingdom will remain and we, if we are members, will survive that shaking. Then God will bring in the new heaven and new earth where righteousness dwells.[17]

17 2 Peter 3:13

When Peter reflects on this, he describes it like this:

> But do not overlook this one fact, beloved, that with the Lord one day is as a thousand years, and a thousand years as one day. The Lord is not slow to fulfil his promise as some count slowness, but is patient toward you, not wishing that any should perish, but that all should reach repentance. But the day of the Lord will come like a thief, and then the heavens will pass away with a roar, and the heavenly bodies will be burned up and dissolved, and the earth and the works that are done on it will be exposed.
>
> Since all these things are thus to be dissolved, what sort of people ought you to be in lives of holiness and godliness, waiting for and hastening the coming of the day of God, because of which the heavens will be set on fire and dissolved, and the heavenly bodies will melt as they burn! (2 Pet 3:8-12)

What sort of people should we be? Holy and godly, because we are looking forward to the new creation! John puts it like this:

> See what kind of love the Father has given to us, that we should be called children of God; and so we are. The reason why the world does not know us is that it did not know him. Beloved, we are God's children now, and what we will be has not yet appeared; but we know that when he appears we shall be like him, because we shall see him as he is. (1 John 3:1-2)

Did you notice it? "*We shall be like him.*"

A person said to me, "How long will it take for me to be a really Christlike person?"

I answered, "A lifetime".

They said "What if I am a late starter?"

I said, "It will still take a lifetime".

It doesn't matter when you started, it will take the rest of your life under your discipline and God's discipline. It takes all our life and it reaches a great climax in the miracle that God performs on us at the last day. We will be Christlike and that is a very good reason for not giving up.

When the Lord Jesus returns, he will bring the process to completion. Unbelievable as it may sound, I will be just like Jesus. That will be a great miracle. Do you wish to know another? You will be, too!

It might be today that this event will take place. We don't know when, but we do know that it will happen. All the work of throwing away the things that are getting in the way, and the work of fighting against temptation, will come to an end.

We mustn't complain when God disciplines us. He is doing a great work in us. I heard a story of an artist whose daughter asked him to draw her something. He quickly dashed off a drawing of the cat lying on the hearth rug, and she was delighted with the result. However, if he was doing a serious painting that was destined to be hung, for example, in the National Gallery, he would have spent considerably more time on it. It would need to withstand the scrutiny of appreciative but careful and critical viewing.

When God works upon us, he is not dashing off a quick cat. He is creating a masterpiece that will be the admiration of millions of people for the whole of eternity. How they will marvel, "That sinful man has been made to reflect the character of the Lord Jesus Christ! What a marvellous thing that is."

What is more, he invites us to cooperate in the process. He says:

> Therefore lift your drooping hands and strengthen your weak knees, and make straight paths for your feet ... (Heb 12:12-13)

It is as if he is saying to us, "Don't give up. There is a great work to be done. There is no doubt what the end product will be. Hang in!"

You can see how essential it is to have our focus on that end goal so that we will not get discouraged.

Whatever happens, do not listen to those people who can offer you the end before it arrives. They won't say it like that. They will say something like, "God doesn't want you to suffer. If you trust him, he will heal you of all your diseases." Do you see how they have offered you the new creation before it is time to go there? They may say, "God wants you to be healthy, wealthy and wise, and it can be yours now". Don't believe it. If you have the end now, there is nothing to look forward to. It is a terrible price to pay. Remember that God has committed himself to making us Christlike and he will bring everything to pass which will accomplish that.[18]

Is it worth the effort?

If you take your eyes off Jesus, you may well ask the question, "Is it worth the effort?" Let me remind you of a passage we read at the beginning of this chapter.

> Then I saw a new heaven and a new earth, for the first heaven and the first earth had passed away, and the sea was no more. And I saw the holy city, new Jerusalem, coming down out of heaven from God, prepared as a bride adorned for her husband. And I heard a loud voice from the throne saying, "Behold, the dwelling place of God is with man. He will dwell with them, and they will be his people, and God himself will be with them as their God. He will wipe away every tear from their eyes, and death shall be no more, neither shall there be mourning nor crying nor pain anymore, for the former things have passed away."
>
> And he who was seated on the throne said, "Behold, I am making all things new". Also he said, "Write this down, for these words are trustworthy and true". And he said to me, "It is done! I am the Alpha and the Omega, the beginning and the end.

18 Romans 8:28ff

> To the thirsty I will give from the spring of the water of life without payment. The one who conquers will have this heritage, and I will be his God and he will be my son. But as for the cowardly, the faithless, the detestable, as for murderers, the sexually immoral, sorcerers, idolaters, and all liars, their portion will be in the lake that burns with fire and sulphur, which is the second death."
>
> Then came one of the seven angels who had the seven bowls full of the seven last plagues and spoke to me, saying, "Come, I will show you the Bride, the wife of the Lamb". And he carried me away in the Spirit to a great, high mountain, and showed me the holy city Jerusalem coming down out of heaven from God, having the glory of God, its radiance like a most rare jewel, like a jasper, clear as crystal. It had a great, high wall, with twelve gates, and at the gates twelve angels, and on the gates the names of the twelve tribes of the sons of Israel were inscribed—on the east three gates, on the north three gates, on the south three gates, and on the west three gates. And the wall of the city had twelve foundations, and on them were the twelve names of the twelve apostles of the Lamb. (Rev 21:1-14)

The bride of Christ is dressed beautifully for her husband. It is God who is making everything new.

He who overcomes will inherit all this. Some will be excluded, so see that you are not one of them.

John wonderfully finishes his vision with these words:

> And I saw no temple in the city, for its temple is the Lord God the Almighty and the Lamb. And the city has no need of sun or moon to shine on it, for the glory of God gives it light, and its lamp is the Lamb. By its light will the nations walk, and the kings of the earth will bring their glory into it, and its gates will never be shut by day—and there will be no night there. They will bring into it the glory and the honour of the nations. But nothing unclean will ever enter it, nor anyone who does what is detestable or false, but only those who are written in the Lamb's book of life. (Rev 21:22-27)

There will be nothing in this new creation to ruin it like there is in our current creation. There will be no sin at all. God is getting us ready to share it with him and with each other. At present, because it has not yet arrived, we are always in a sense dissatisfied. This is how it is described in Romans 8:

> For we know that the whole creation has been groaning together in the pains of childbirth until now. And not only the creation, but we ourselves, who have the firstfruits of the Spirit, groan inwardly as we wait eagerly for adoption as sons, the redemption of our bodies. For in this hope we were saved. Now hope that is seen is not hope. For who hopes for what he sees? But if we hope for what we do not see, we wait for it with patience. (Rom 8:22-25)

Please notice that we are groaning with the whole

creation because our bodies have not yet been redeemed. Sure, we have been forgiven, we have been made friends with God, we have received the Holy Spirit who is faithfully working away in accordance with the Father's plan, but we have not yet received the new bodies. Therefore, we are not fitted for the new creation yet.

Let us finish by returning to Hebrews 12:

> ... "Yet once more I will shake not only the earth but also the heavens." This phrase, "Yet once more", indicates the removal of things that are shaken—that is, things that have been made—in order that the things that cannot be shaken may remain. Therefore let us be grateful for receiving a kingdom that cannot be shaken, and thus let us offer to God acceptable worship, with reverence and awe, for our God is a consuming fire. (Heb 12:26-29)

You will remember when we looked before we noted what it was that cannot be shaken—it was those who belonged to the kingdom. They are unshakable.

Because of this, the writer tells us to "be grateful ... and offer to God acceptable worship, with reverence and awe".

It is the mark of the pagans that they do not thank God.[19] In the light of all that God has done for us and all that he will still do, we should be thankful.

19 Romans 1:21

We are called upon to worship God "acceptably". It is important that we should not equate worship simply with going to church. Worship is obeying God because he is God. Every act of obedience is an act of worship. It is when we present our bodies as living sacrifices that we worship acceptably.[20]

Finally we are reminded that "God is a consuming fire". We have already been introduced to the idea that God will judge the whole world as he sieves out everything that is not good and godly.

Conclusion

Because there is a great heritage for the children of God, we are to be people who are straining to grow in holiness. Our eyes are fixed on the Lord Jesus who is both our leader and example. He did not grow weary or give up in his great sin-bearing work, but he carried it out completely.

Ponder your place in the New Creation, where you will be sinless like the Lord Jesus and your environment will be sin-free. We are to see that we are well-equipped for the great day that Jesus appears.

If it is today, will he find you in a tracksuit with your hair looking like a bird nested in it? Or will he find you as the bride, beautifully dressed for her bridegroom?

20 Romans 12:1-2

HOLINESS

4. One sinner's testimony: the first 60 years are the hardest!

I WAS CONVERTED IN 1947. I am writing this in 2005, which means I have been a Christian for nearly 60 years. It is a long time in which to give something a try. For me the best description of how I feel with regard to holiness is summed up by the quote of the apostle Paul in Philippians 3:

> [I want to know] him and the power of his resurrection, and ... share his sufferings, becoming like him in his death, that by any means possible I may attain the resurrection from the dead.
>
> Not that I have already obtained this or am already perfect, but I press on to make it my own, because Christ Jesus has made me his own. Brothers, I do not consider that I have made it my own. But one

> thing I do: forgetting what lies behind and straining forward to what lies ahead, I press on toward the goal for the prize of the upward call of God in Christ Jesus. (Phil 3:10-14)

When I became a Christian, I knew very little about what would be involved in living the Christian life. I knew that God was there. I knew that he had sent his Son into the world and that through the death and resurrection of the Lord Jesus I could be saved from the right judgement of God on my sinful life. I realized that I was to live a life in obedience to my new Master. At the time the theory of this seemed elementary, and the Christian walk seemed such an easy thing to keep going with. The reality was that it turned out to be much more difficult than I had thought. Please don't misunderstand me, however. Becoming a Christian has been the best thing that has ever happened to me. It is wonderful to know that Jesus is present with me all the time by his Spirit. It is great to know that my sins are forgiven and that I will be part of the New Creation. It is deeply reassuring to know that God will guide me in the paths of righteousness for his name's sake.

But having said that, I must admit that the day-to-day seeking to live in obedience to Jesus has been very difficult. How I long to be holy and to be just like the Lord Jesus Christ! Achieving it is a different matter!

Instant and effortless holiness

Because daily obedience to Jesus is difficult to do, and because we long for holiness, we can be easy prey for people who offer an instantaneous method of sanctification.

During my time as a Christian, several alternatives have been offered to me either for holiness itself or as different methods of attaining it. So I thought it might be good to write something about them, as a warning not to waste time pursuing them as I have.

One of these was built on a misunderstanding of Romans 6:

> For the death he died he died to sin, once for all, but the life he lives he lives to God. So you also must consider yourselves dead to sin and alive to God in Christ Jesus.
>
> Let not sin therefore reign in your mortal bodies, to make you obey their passions. Do not present your members to sin as instruments for unrighteousness, but present yourselves to God as those who have been brought from death to life, and your members to God as instruments for righteousness. For sin will have no dominion over you, since you are not under law but under grace. (Rom 6:10-14)

It was suggested to me that Jesus had died to sin and that therefore we were to reckon ourselves "dead to sin". It followed, according to this argument, that if we trusted in Jesus, we would be impervious to the pull of sin upon our lives. All we had to do was to rest in the promises of God, and we would always experience victory over temptation.

The instantaneousness and effortlessness of this theory was irresistible to me. I took to it like a duck to water! However the truth of the matter is that the theory was wrong, and because it was wrong, it did not work. It flew in the face of so many other parts of the Bible and it was a misunderstanding of the passage. Jesus did not die to the *effect* of sin. He died to the *penalty* of sin. That is what I was to 'count' (as referred to in verse 11). I was to consider that I had died to the penalty of sin. This becomes the motivation to resist temptation and surrender myself to God. I was to be active in this and not a passive onlooker.

This false teaching left scars on me for a long time. My friends told me that they were experiencing continuous victory over temptation, which discouraged me greatly because I wasn't. It made matters worse that I lied to them by telling them I, too, was experiencing a victory that in reality I wasn't (and they weren't).

I heard a story which deserves to be true, of a man insisting to his friend that he was experiencing wonderful, constant victory over sin. As he was speaking, his wife was behind him shaking her head as if to say, "Don't believe it. He isn't anything of the sort!"

The fact was that to anyone close to us, the claim that we were experiencing complete victory over sin, to the extent that we never sinned, was clearly a fabrication.

It was a gloomy time in my Christian walk. After a time, God delivered me from it. In his providence, I was moved to a different part of Australia. As I evaluated and reflected on my experience, I realized that I had been wrong, and I determined that from that time on, I would always try and be honest about what was happening to me.

I was greatly encouraged by these verses in Philippians 2:

> Therefore, my beloved, as you have always obeyed, so now, not only as in my presence but much more in my absence, *work out your own salvation with fear and trembling, for it is God who works in you,* both to will and to work for his good pleasure.
>
> Do all things without grumbling or questioning, that you may be blameless and innocent, children of God without blemish in the midst of a crooked and twisted generation, among whom you shine as lights in the world, holding fast to the word of life, so that in the day of Christ I may be proud that I did not run in vain or labour in vain. (Phil 2:12-16, my italics)

I am to work at my salvation because God is at work. It is not an either/or. It is a both/and. God is at work and I am to work. The term 'continue to work' in verse 13 is sometimes used of hard physical work; the sort of work where the perspiration rolls down and the shower beckons.

The same results of instantaneous sanctification and

effortless obedience were offered to me if I were to be 'baptised by the Holy Spirit' as a different and subsequent experience to my conversion. But since I had been so badly hurt by my previous experience, I decided on this occasion to examine the Bible more closely. When I did this, I discovered that this view of baptism in the Holy Spirit was not what the Bible was teaching at all. This is neither the time nor the place to correct this error. It is sufficient to say that the baptism of the Holy Spirit is what happens to people when they are converted, and that without the Holy Spirit we should not be looking for subsequent blessing, so much as asking God to help us understand the gospel for the first time.

Alternatives to holiness

Because obedience does require effort, many people are attracted to false alternatives to the life-long quest for holiness. Consider some of the following:

1. Being in love with the world

One of the saddest passages in scripture comes toward the end of 2 Timothy 4:

> Do your best to come to me soon. For Demas, in love with this present world, has deserted me and gone to Thessalonica. Crescens has gone to Galatia,

> Titus to Dalmatia. Luke alone is with me. Get Mark and bring him with you, for he is very useful to me for ministry. (2 Tim 4:9-11)

You will remember that the apostle Paul is in prison in Rome. He is lonely and longs for Timothy to visit him. For various reasons, good and not-so-good, his friends have left him.

Demas is one of those friends. He has abandoned the apostle because, in Paul's simple words, "he loved this world".

Some Christians have just given up in the quest for holiness. They have drifted back to the old way of life. They are indistinguishable in their lifestyle from the people around them who are not really Christians at all. Life here and now has become too good. It has become too full of ease and comfort. Change could threaten this. It might even cause us to undergo persecution for Jesus' sake.

If you are under pressure to give up in this way, may I simply urge you to repent quickly, and start following Jesus again.

2. Becoming rich

Even as I write this, there are people in our world who are preaching a 'prosperity gospel'. They reason that God wants the best for us and that if we are generous givers we will be generous receivers from God. They argue that God wants us to be wealthy, as well as healthy and wise—possibly even in that order!

This idea flies in the face of so much teaching of our Lord on money and how easily riches can deceive us.[21] We should reject it for the deception that it is. I cannot think of a single reason why God would want me to be rich; unless it was so I could give my wealth away to those in need and especially for the spread of the gospel. We can be sure that in the new creation there will be as many good things as we can handle and plenty of time to pursue what now in this life we cannot pursue.

3. Neglecting holiness for other alternatives

I think it is possible to stress some aspects of the Christian life so much that holiness just gets neglected. I think I have seen some Christians whose obsession with evangelism leads them to neglect the development of their Christlike character. They have failed to pay attention to the advice the apostle Paul gives to Titus about how he is to instruct slaves to behave. In Titus 2, Paul says:

> Slaves are to be submissive to their own masters in everything; they are to be well-pleasing, not argumentative, not pilfering, but showing all good faith, so that in everything they may adorn the doctrine of God our Saviour. (Titus 2:9-10)

21 Mark 10:23-25; Luke 8:14

Holiness, then, does not compete with evangelism. Holiness enhances evangelism.

I think I have also observed this out-of-kilter version of the Christian life in some people engaged in the healing ministry. They are so obsessed with it that it becomes the be-all and end-all of the Christian life.

Holiness will require effort

Holiness will require effort because of the world, the flesh, and the devil.

When I was a child, I did something that nowadays would be regarded as distinctly old-fashioned—that is, I learned the Catechism from the *1662 Anglican Book of Common Prayer*. One of the questions in the Catechism asks about the promises my Godparents made on my behalf. The answer is:

> They did promise and vow three things in my name. First, that I should renounce the devil and all his works, the pomps and vanity of this wicked world, and all the sinful lusts of the flesh.

It is true that at age 7 I didn't have a clue what "the pomps and vanity of this wicked world" might be, to say nothing of the "sinful lusts of the flesh"! However, as I grew up, I soon learned by bitter experience.

There are agencies at work to prevent us from being holy. The Bible says in 1 Peter 5:

> [Cast] all your anxieties on him, because he cares for you. Be sober-minded; be watchful. Your adversary the devil prowls around like a roaring lion, seeking someone to devour. Resist him, firm in your faith, knowing that the same kinds of suffering are being experienced by your brotherhood throughout the world. (1 Pet 5:7-9)

We should not be terrified by the fact that the devil will seek to divert us. We are to resist him and he will flee from us. Remember that the One who dwells with us is more powerful than the devil.

Another agency seeking to divert us from godly living is the world we live in—a world that, by and large, neglects God and thinks about life as if God was not there at all. This philosophy of life has no place for God. It is often referred to in the Bible by the term 'the world'. Notice the warning in 1 John 2:

> Do not love the world or the things in the world. If anyone loves the world, the love of the Father is not in him. For all that is in the world—the desires of the flesh and the desires of the eyes and pride in possessions—is not from the Father but is from the world. (1 John 2:15-16)

It is a strong warning. This worldly thinking is very appealing to the sinful person because it panders to our pride. We love the idea that we know and can understand life without God and his help. It is foolish, but nonetheless appealing. Don't do it.

The third agency at work against us is our own sinful nature. We have been set free from slavery to sin and have been set free to be obedient to God. We are to refuse the desires we know are wrong and we are to choose to do what is right.[22]

Holiness is progressive

All of us would like to be made instantly like the Lord Jesus Christ. In the early part of my Christian experience I used to think I found it hard to be godly because I was new at it. However, I have been a Christian for so long that I cannot use that excuse any longer.

I have been helped by the verse in 2 Corinthians 3 that says:

> And we all, with unveiled face, beholding the glory of the Lord, are being transformed into the same image from one degree of glory to another. For this comes from the Lord who is the Spirit. (2 Cor 3:18)

Holiness is progressive. God promises us that it will develop in us over the course of time.

From time to time I have met Christian people in whom the Christlike character was well developed. I must say they were very appealing people. I was so

22 Galatians 5:16-26

encouraged to know that what was happening in their lives, God had promised to do in mine. I am to be patient and co-operate to the best of my ability with this process. If I dwell on the times when I fall and am disobedient, I tend to get discouraged. However, I am to look to the Lord Jesus and be encouraged by the promise that God, who never goes back on his word, has promised to make me just like him.

If the first 60 years feel like the hardest, then we should be assured and comforted that this is because they are. But they will seem like nothing in eternity, and we will be able to see that Paul was right when he said:

> For this light momentary affliction is preparing for us an eternal weight of glory beyond all comparison, as we look not to the things that are seen but to the things that are unseen. For the things that are seen are transient, but the things that are unseen are eternal. (2 Cor 4:17-18)

DISCUSSION GUIDE

The questions on the following pages are designed to help you discuss the content of *A Sinner's Guide to Holiness* with others—your spouse, or a friend, or the small group you meet with at church. Use these questions as a way of talking back over the content of each chapter, and encouraging each other to put God's word into practice.

Chapter 1 — Holiness: Where it begins

1. What do you immediately think of when you hear the word 'holiness'? Is this accurate when compared to how the Bible speaks of it?

Read back over Job 38 (on pp. 15-16), Job 42:1-6 (on p. 17), Isaiah 6:1-7 (on pp. 20-21) and Revelation 1:9-18 (on pp. 24-25) before answering the following questions.

2. What aspects of God's character and nature struck you from these passages?
3. What are the reactions of the people mentioned, and what do they teach you about how you should respond to God?
4. Why should we seek holiness?

5. What does God do to help people who want to be holy as he is?
6. In response to what God has done, how do we begin a life of holiness?

Pray that God will make you holy.

Chapter 2 — Holiness: How it progresses

1. Why isn't it enough for Christians just to be forgiven their sins?
2. What makes it hard to continue to work at holiness?
3. Look again at Hebrews 12:1-17 (on pp. 39, 47, 50, 52).
   - What commands are given concerning holiness?
   - What examples?
   - What encouragements?
   - What warnings?
4. Read Romans 8:28-30 (on pp. 37-38). How do these verses help us understand the place of suffering in our lives, and how it leads to holiness?
5. What areas of your holiness do you need to work on?

Use the answers to these questions as a basis for prayer.

Chapter 3 — Holiness: Its fulfilment

1. Having read this chapter, give your impressions of what heaven will be like. How much is heaven a feature of your thinking? Is this good or bad? Why or why not?

2. Read Hebrews 12:18-29 (on pp. 59-60, 71). In what ways will heaven be like the experience of Israel at Mt Sinai? In what ways will it be different? What part does the word of God play in both gatherings?
3. Look back at Revelation 21:1-14 (on pp. 68-69).
   - What will the day of judgement be like?
   - What will the basis of judgement be?

   (You might like to refer back to Hebrews 12 too.)
4. What incentives have we been given in this chapter for working at holiness?

Pray that you will be more mindful of heaven.

Chapter 4 — The first 60 years are the hardest

1. What is your personal testimony about living the Christian life—is it hard or easy?
2. What shortcuts or alternatives to holiness have you heard of or been tempted to take?
3. Re-read Philippians 2:12-16 (p. 77) and Philippians 3:10-14 (on pp. 73-74).
   - What expectations do they give concerning the Christian life?
   - What encouragements or instructions do they give about how to continue?
4. What obstacles stand in the way of holiness?
5. What guarantees do we have concerning the future? (See 2 Corinthians 3:18, 4:17-18 on pp. 83-84.)

6. Thinking back over the whole book, how would you summarize the key ideas and encouragements to someone who said: “Give me a two minute book review”?

   Pray about applying the ideas you have learnt.

matthiasmedia

Matthias Media is an independent, evangelical, non-denominational company based in Sydney, Australia. We produce an extensive range of Bible studies, books, Bible reading materials, evangelistic tools, training resources, periodicals and multimedia resources. In all that we do, our mission is:

> To serve our Lord Jesus Christ, and the growth of his gospel in Australia and the world, by producing and delivering high quality, Bible-based resources.

For more information about our resources, and to browse our online catalogue, visit our website:

www.matthiasmedia.com.au

How to buy our resources

1. At Christian bookstores everywhere

2. Direct over the internet:
   – in the UK and Europe: www.thegoodbook.co.uk
   – in the US: www.matthiasmedia.com
   – in Australia and rest of the world: www.matthiasmedia.com.au

3. Direct by phone:
   – within Australia: 1800 814 360 (Sydney: 9663 1478)
   – international: + 61 2 9663 1478
   – within UK: 0845 225 0880

4. Trade enquiries:
   – email us: sales@matthiasmedia.com.au

Know and Tell the Gospel

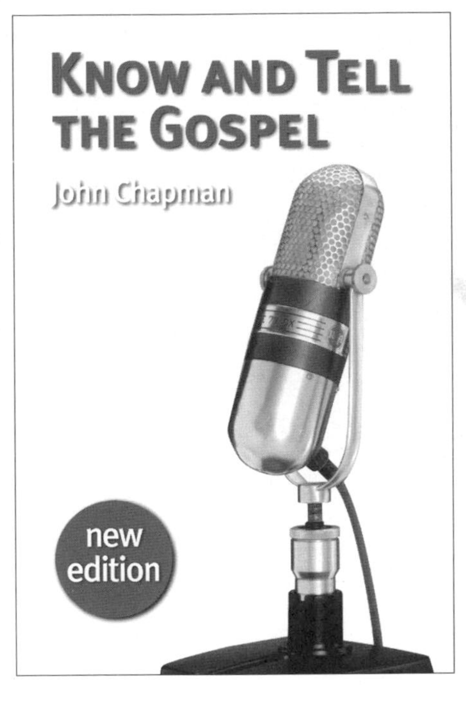

Know and Tell the Gospel deals with all the questions that so quickly come to mind when we think about sharing our faith. Just what is the gospel anyway? Is it my job to explain it to people? What is God's role and what is mine? Where does church fit in? Why is evangelism so often hard? And how can we train ourselves and others to be involved?

In his characteristically friendly and engaging way, 'Chappo' provides warm encouragement, insightful biblical teaching, and a wealth of practical information on evangelism for all Christians. This new edition has been extensively revised and re-written, and contains up-to-date information and evaluation on current resources for evangelism.

Beyond Greed

'Greed' is not the most fashionable concept these days. It ranks with 'guilt' and 'sin' as words that many modern people have virtually stopped using.

According to Brian Rosner, greed is also a massive blind spot for Christians, which is surprising given how much the Bible has to say about it. He writes:

"The most disturbing thing about the fact that greed is idolatry is that hardly anybody owns up to being a worshipper. Imagine the response of disbelief in the local church if it were revealed that the vast majority of its members were secretly worshipping other gods. Yet if our analysis of the religion of money is right, the unthinkable may not be so far from the truth."

Beyond Greed helps open our eyes to the problems, and proposes a liberating lifestyle that trades in greed and materialism for something of far greater worth and satisfaction.

For more information or to order contact:

Matthias Media
Telephone: +61 2 9663 1478 | Facsimile: +61 2 9663 3265
Email: sales@matthiasmedia.com.au

www.matthiasmedia.com.au